# NO LONGER TRAPPED

*An Unapologetic Guide to Recover from Trauma, Reclaim Your Life and Unleash Purpose*

BY

Dr. Shelita McGowan

All rights reserved.
This book, or parts thereof, may not be reproduced, distributed, transmitted in any form, by any means, without permission in writing from the author.

Copyright © 2023 Dr. Shelita McGowan

Published by
Live Limitless Media Group
Publishing@sierrarainge.com
info@livelimitlessmedia.com

Dr. Shelita McGowan
Contact Information:
Email: drshelita@gmail.com
Website: www.drshelitamcgowan.com

Printed in the United States of America

Cover Design by: Budi Detika

ISBN: 978-1-952903-38-0

# TABLE OF CONTENTS

Dedication ..................................................................... v

Acknowledgements ..................................................... vii

Introduction .................................................................. 1

**Chapter One:** Slow Dancing with Fear ..................... 27

**Chapter Two:** Navigating Series of Losses ............... 37

**Chapter Three:** New Healing For Old Wounds
Embracing Healing and Finding Freedom .................. 51

**Chapter Four:** Reclaiming Peace, Purpose
and Personal Power ...................................................... 61

**Chapter Five:** "The Test of Trusting Again" ............ 71

**Chapter Six:** "Do a New Dance"
Designing a New Vision For Your Life ....................... 83

**Chapter Seven:** Daring To Do a New Dance ............ 97

No Longer Trapped Daily Affirmations ................... 103

No Longer Trapped Devotions and Journal Prompts 109

About the Author ...................................................... 118

NO LONGER TRAPPED

# DEDICATION

This book is dedicated to my husband, Dr. Royce McGowan, and my three children Kennedi, Christian, and Addisyn. Your constant love and unwavering care continues to inspire me to heal, grow, thrive and evolve. I love you.

NO LONGER TRAPPED

# ACKNOWLEDGEMENTS

I would like to thank God for giving me the strength to release the fear I harbored inside for years and for granting me the courage to write this book to help and inspire others.

I would like to thank special friends who shared their gift of time to mentor me as I wrote this book, especially when I would stall, you would push me to keep going. Thank you to everyone who is committed to helping others become their authentic selves and only want them to live in true happiness. The world is a better place because of individuals like you who want to unselfishly give and mentor others. You are the special friends I call my bright shining stars.

To all the people I have had the opportunity to care for as patients, to lead in some way, or be led or mentored by, or those whom I watch your greatness and strength from afar, I would like to say thank you for being inspirations to write this book and tell my story unapologetically.

To my crew, you have been with me during some highs and lows, but you stuck with me through it all. I shared with some of you how I've always wanted to write a book and it's finally here. You ladies have all played a significant part in my healing. Thank you for always listening, always acknowledging my random texts, and for being my friends unconditionally. I don't know where I would be without my crew.

Royce, thank you for always being there for me. Thank you for being the selfless God fearing leader of our family. Thank you for providing me with love, understanding, and support.

## Acknowledgements

To my children, remember mommy loves you more than anything. This book is dedicated to you, to remind you that no matter what you go through, life can get better. Trust God and remember if God did it for me, He's able to do it for you too. Always remember to lean on God.

To my parents, Pastor Chris and Priscilla, I love you and thank you for always believing in me.

To my brothers, Ryan and Tony, I love you both. My niece's Bayleigh and Brielle and my beautiful sister in law Brooke, I love you.

Shantel, thank you for always reminding me to focus on what's in front of me, instead of behind and always being available when I need you and even when I didn't know I needed you. You were there.

Kiandra and staff, I appreciate you all for everything you do. We are in this together.

To all who have gone through a traumatic experience, may you find healing and remember you are not what you have been through. You are loved.

# INTRODUCTION

*"And after you have suffered a little while, the God of all grace, who has called you to his eternal glory in Christ, will himself restore, confirm, strengthen, and establish you."*
**~ Peter 5:10**

There are some moments in life that completely shake you to your core. These life altering instances have a way of disrupting your sense of normalcy, leaving you left with fragments of who you once were. What do you do when life throws you a curveball and not only does it wreak havoc in your life, but it bruises your heart, taunts your mind and wounds your soul. How do you handle the disdain of grief that lingers? What is the remedy to recover from trauma and navigate the grief that accommodates disruption? I have always been a woman who sought God in times of trouble and petitioned for wisdom during seasons when I was being tested. I've grown to learn that God often uses the duality of pain and purpose to position us to operate in greater power. This is evident in our lives when a situation that once created chaos in our hearts and minds can transcend trauma and become the foundation of our faith, fueling us to make a positive impact in the lives of others. While the journey from pain to purpose is a bumpy pathway with many crossroads, you realize that as you navigate the tough terrain of your life's test, you hold the power to claim the victory even when you've been victimized in the most violent way.

My husband and I had recently returned home from a cruise and this was our first day back at work. On this particular day, we were working in separate clinics. He was at the main clinic and I was taking patients at my satellite clinic. I can remember so vividly when two men

## Introduction

entered the clinic lobby. One of them had been in some sort of physical altercation and was wearing the bruises on his face. When they entered the lobby, one of the men took a seat while the other approached me looking for my husband. Something felt eerie about my interaction with him, however he had been a previous patient so I wasn't afraid to talk to him. I found his questions concerning the whereabouts of my husband to be very strange since my husband was known to always work at our main clinic location. This patient in particular knew that and I even said to him, "you know he's not here." I glanced over at the guy who was seated in the lobby and I noticed that he seemed to have intentionally pulled his hat all the way down in an attempt to conceal his face. It was something about his demeanor and disposition that I will never forget. I asked them to leave in a professional way and suggested they go to the main clinic to receive treatment.

One week later, we would have another encounter, this one changing the trajectory of all of our lives. It was approximately 9:12 am. I was sitting on the toilet when I was startled by a loud noise along with my mother's panic fueled screams. I remember the details of this day with clarity and precision; not only because it changed my life, but because I found myself reliving the traumatic experiences that transpired every day for 14 years.

When I think back, everything about that day was outside of my normal routine. I left my clinic early to drop off documents to my attorney. I would normally have my assistant do this for me, but on this particular day, I decided to take care of it myself. After leaving the attorney's office, I went home before heading back to the clinic. I had to pick up my daughter and bring her to a doctor's appointment. I pulled into my driveway and I parked in front of my house. Normally, I would drive to the back of my home and park my car in the garage

## Introduction

where I would enter my home from the back door. I remember it being a beautiful day. The sky was clear and the sun was shining brightly. The bright blue skies certainly didn't suggest that my life was about to be catapulted into disarray. I stopped my car in the driveway, got out and walked down my sidewalk to my front door. I was on the phone talking to my cousin about the cruise we had just returned from. I didn't notice anything different in my surroundings. I used the key to my front door which I never used since I rarely entered through the front door. I walked in and went straight to my bathroom. I didn't even let my mother know I had come inside. As soon as I sat down on the toilet, I heard a loud bang, almost like an explosion, accompanied by my mother's frightful screams that startled me. I was still on the phone with my cousin at the time, she too was startled from the noise and worriedly asked, "what was that?!!" I reacted immediately, I don't recall where the phone went or how we ended the call. What I do remember was jumping up from the toilet and making my way towards the sound of my mother's screams. As I ran from the restroom, my purple-colored scrubs along with my panties were still at my ankles. I was attempting to pull them up, while running to my mother, and when I turned the corner I was met with an armed and unmasked intruder who forcibly pressed the barrel of his nine-millimeter gun in the center of my forehead with great pressure. He then grabbed me by my hair, turned me around and put me in a chokehold. The intruder had his elbow pressed into my neck, while the pressure of his gun pierced my forehead. My airway was restricted, my breaths were interrupted and my vagina was exposed due to me not being able to properly secure my clothing. As the intruder erratically made his way around the room, my exposed body dangled while being constricted by the death grip he had around my neck. While dragging me toward my kitchen where my mom and three year old daughter were, he directed his rage towards my mom and

## Introduction

told her to shut up and he demanded that she make my daughter shut up as well. My daughter was crying and screaming. I told my daughter to be quiet. He kept saying he would kill my baby. "Don't make me pop the baby! Make it shut up" he screamed. I was fighting to breathe through his chokehold and I found myself going from extreme panic to full out fear paralysis. I was overwhelmed with the uttermost fear and trying not to disassociate from the shock. Frustrated by my daughter's cries, he removed the gun from my head, and he pointed it at my baby. A vision I will never unsee. I plead with despair, "mom please get her to be quiet." In that very moment, my fear intensified and my entire focus shifted towards my daughter's safety. My mother frantically tried to console my daughter and the unmasked gunman placed his gun back to my head.

He never loosened his grip around my neck. I was hanging on to his forearm desperately trying to grasp for pockets of air. While I struggled to breathe, snot, tears, sweat and blood ran down my face. As he dragged me from the kitchen. He made my mother and daughter follow us to the family room. We passed by my foyer where I saw another intruder standing with a bandana over his face. He appeared to be on guard. I could see my front door from my foyer and I noticed that it had a huge hole that had been kicked through the center of it. Fragments of wood were all over the floor. The door never came off the hinges. It was solely a gigantic hole in the bottom of the door.

It was clear that whatever the men had come for, they would stop at nothing to get it. My voice trembled with a desperate fear as I asked them what they wanted. I noticed my purse sitting on the sofa and I begged them to take it. He yelled, "I don't want your purse." He then grabbed me by my hair, and turned me around to face another direction. When I looked up, I saw a third intruder ripping through the linen closet in my bathroom. I could hear my heart thrusting inside my chest as I scanned the room with my eyes to see if there were any more men. That's when I noticed my gun sitting on my mantel. Although it was somewhat within reach, there wasn't much I could do. I was outnumbered and overpowered. My assailant flung me around again, this time knocking my glasses off of my face. He kept hitting my right temporal area of my face with the gun. Over and over again. He began to drag me into my bedroom yelling for me to tell him where the money was. I asked him what money? He yelled again, after hitting my head once more, "tell me where the money is!" I told him my husband had a safe. He yelled, "where is it?" The intruder in the linen closet then said, "tell us where the money is Doc!" When he called me Doc, I became even more afraid. I told him it was in my husband's closet and he yanked me in that direction. If he would have demanded the combination to the safe, I would probably not be writing this book today. The truth is that I had no idea what the combination was. When we made it into my husband's closet, the third intruder who had been ram shacking my closet followed us. He squatted in the closet to move the clothes out of the way in an attempt to find the safe. He now had his face directly in front of my bare vagina. My panties and purple scrub pants were still around my ankles. The thought of him seeing the most intimate parts of my body was both humiliating and degrading. Although the men didn't sexually assault me, the physical and mental violation I endured while in the vulnerability of my nakedness made me feel extremely exploited. Three strange men who had violently entered my home at gunpoint now knew what my private areas looked like.

They found the safe in the closet and the third intruder picked it up. As he lifted the safe, he paused and looked at me in my face as if they were deciding what to do with me now that they had what they were looking for. No words were spoken in that brief moment. The intruder who had the gun to my head then became even

## Introduction

more enraged. They got what they wanted but he was angrier. The yelling, cussing and choking became more intense as we were exiting the closet. That's when I felt a gust of wind come into my house. As the wind breezed by, I heard a small voice from within whisper instructions to lay hands on the gunmen who still had me in a chokehold and pray for him. I must have been falling back into a state of fear paralysis when I envisioned my lifeless body laying in a pool of blood in my foyer. It was an image that has stuck with me. It is still so vivid today that I can thoroughly illustrate it on paper. I realized that the men didn't intend to take the safe and leave, and I saw a vision of myself in the aftermath of my demise. It was like an out of body experience. I snapped back into the troubling reality of the present moment when the voice that was first a whisper was now more assertive and urging me to place my hands on my attacker and begin to pray for him. Because of the way that I was now positioned, I was able to reach around him and place my hands on his back as I prayed out loud for God to forgive him. I rubbed his back in a calming fashion as I prayed for him. I didn't pray for God to save my life, or the life of my mother and daughter, instead I prayed that God would grant him grace and mercy. I asked God to forgive him. He became irritated and increasingly angered by my prayers. He yelled, "shut up! Shut up bitch, Be quiet! Shut the fuck up! I don't need you to pray for me!" He then dragged me out of my bedroom with one arm around my neck and his gun still to my head. He yanked the phone from the wall, and threw it towards the ground shattering it on our marble floors. He pulled every phone he could find out of the wall and slammed them all into the floor so that we couldn't call for help. As he dragged me back to the foyer, the gunmen with the bandana covering his face was still standing on guard. When I made eye contact with him, he became grossly familiar. He reminded me of the strange man who had visited my clinic the previous week with a former patient looking

## Introduction

for my husband. He then nodded his head at the gunman who was holding me hostage. He seemed a bit panicked and confused as he continued to shake his head motioning "No" to his partner in crime. The guy who had the gun to my head appeared to be confused when he said, "No! We're going to leave her?" The masked man replied and said, "let's go!" The guy who had the gun to my head seemed to not understand why the man who had a bandana covering his mouth was nodding no and saying, "let's go." He then took me by my hair and slammed my face into a glass table as hard as he possibly could and then ran out of my house. The impact of my face slamming through the table was so forceful that my face was bruised black, blue and purple for weeks. When the three men exited the home through the hole in the door, I crawled to the window and watched them get into a vehicle. I pulled up my panties and scrub bottoms. As soon as I thought we were in the clear, I called my husband immediately. My first thought was him and right after I called the police. When the police arrived, they thought I had been pistol whipped due to the bruises and lacerations on my face. A detective was one of the officers who responded to my 911 call. She sat me down, and she told me that when she first received the call of an armed home invasion the first thing in the morning, she assumed that she would be entering a blood bath. She told me that in her years of experience, she had never responded to a call of this nature where there were survivors.

All of the officers stared at me in astonishment. My face was continuing to swell and the first responders were trying to give me ice to help with the swelling. They wanted to know exactly what had happened and how I was able to survive the home invasion. I told them that I didn't know. I told the detective that I prayed for the young man, and deep down in my heart I truly believe that the instance of obedience to the holy spirit that instructed me to lay hands on the young man and pray for him was the reason why my life and the lives of my mom and daughter were spared.

That day completely derailed my life. I relived and replayed every moment of that day in my mind constantly for 14 years. I developed debilitating anxiety, insomnia, paranoia and PTSD that would plague me for years to come.

The assailants were caught after one of their alleged grandmothers anonymously called our home phone to share the locations of the home intruders who she overheard discussing their involvement in the crime. All three were eventually arrested and tried for the crime against me and my family and although they were behind bars, my sense of safety and normalcy would remain completely shattered. The trial proved to be another layer of trauma that forced me to face my attackers in a court of law. I was terrorized and threatened in the courtroom by one of the intruder's family members. There was one instance when one of the home intruders' mothers cornered me in the court restroom. She was upset that I was testifying against her son. She wanted me to drop the charges or request a light sentence on his behalf. She yelled out, "He doesn't deserve to spend his life in prison, it's not like he killed you or that baby. She went on to say, "he has a child too." I was traumatized, torn and my mind was tired. The court security ended up getting me out of the restroom and the family members were banned from the remaining court proceedings in an attempt to protect me from any further attacks. For months police detail would follow me home from work and drive by my house. I no longer felt safe anywhere. Not home, not at work and not even in my own skin. I developed phobias that were triggered by colors, sounds, smells and interactions with strangers. The smell of musk and the stale odor of Black n' Mild's cigarettes taunted me. My airway was overwhelmed with this particular scent as I was cuffed in a chokehold by my attacker. The color purple would trigger emotions of intense fear and unimaginable vulnerability whenever I saw it anywhere. The scrubs that dangled around my ankles exposing my vagina during the attack were purple and I've struggled with securing a sense of safety whenever I see any hues of the color. The violence I experienced that day literally crippled me to my core. It made me an overprotective mom; especially with my oldest daughter. I couldn't handle the thought of anything happening to her and I became the ultimate helicopter mom. We had survived so much.

Since my husband and I were well known and well respected in the community for our clinical work as chiropractors, news of the attack was buzzing throughout the city. Knowing that my attack was the talk of the town intensified my anxiety and leaving home or even leaving my house became a challenge. News reports continued to hit the airways and the trial came to an end which resulted in two of the three men being convicted and sentenced to life in prison. The other assailant received a lesser sentence because he testified against the others. I struggled to even imagine a life of normalcy, let alone truly experience it. News of the home invasion that left a local prominent chiropractor paralyzed by fear gained the interest of Dr. Phil who hosted the most comprehensive forum on mental health issues on the Oprah Winfrey Network. His producers invited me on the show to share my story. I was nervous about discussing it because I was also 10 weeks pregnant at the time. While on stage telling my trauma to the world, another trauma was unfolding. Before going on stage I began to have stomach cramps. I went to the restroom moments prior to walking on stage; in the restroom I noticed a heavy discharge of blood accompanied with severe abdominal pain. I knew in my heart I was having a miscarriage. I told one of the producers and they were so empathetic. I was asked if I wanted to reschedule, and if I needed an ambulance. Their team was eager to help and they made me feel so supported. I informed them that despite the current miscarriage that had transpired, I still wanted to tell my story. On stage, I sat, shared and literally bled out while mustering up all the strength and courage that I could in order to speak my truth and tell my story.

The producers were shocked and a little reluctant when I told them I still wanted to push through and continue with filming the segment but I was so tired of holding all of the fear in. It had already cost me my peace, my joy, my sense of safety and now possibly the life of my unborn child due to all of the ongoing stress that my body was constantly under. After filming, I traveled back home to process yet another loss. I cried at the thought of losing my baby but sadly, they wouldn't be the last tears that I would shed. I believe my womb was so full of terror that it proved unsafe to carry. I went on to suffer 7 more miscarriages and I believe that it was a direct result of the trauma that I was storing in my body. Although the robbery was over, the trial had ended, and the intruders were behind bars, I struggled to put it all behind me. How could I? That day lived in my dreams and it took over every idle moment in my mind.

Over the years I was still bleeding on the inside. I was bleeding from carrying internal trauma while still smiling, still going out, still trying to function as if nothing was going on. I was embarrassed to talk about my trauma because I felt like somehow I had brought it on myself. The guilt and the shame of a stranger/intruder seeing my naked body coupled with the resentment and anger of feeling hopeless in the moment, along with the grief of losing my sense of safety and the sadness of having my sanity tested consumed me all at once.

If I was ever going to break free from the cycle of recycled pain, I had to learn to listen to God, and trust Him to restore my joy, reignite my passion for living and release me from the shackles of those painful memories. It had been 14 years since the attack when I decided I could no longer afford to be stuck in a rut within my mind allowing my marriage, my relationships with friends and family as well as my overall wellness to suffer.

As a chiropractor, I attended college for approximately eight years. I studied the musculoskeletal system in detail. I even spent two semesters dissecting deceased bodies. I learned about trauma and how it can physically manifest into disease, illnesses and disorders, but I never imagined that it would be me.

Trauma can be stored in the jaw, pelvic floor (hip area) and the diaphragm. The pain in these areas comes from our misplaced emotions while symptoms of stiff neck are often a result of tension. We often fail to connect the dots between our emotional distress and our physical dis-ease. We fail to recognize the physical pain that results from emotional and mental trauma because it doesn't leave a scar; the wound is internal but the pain manifests physically. This clinical hyperawareness along with internal turmoil slowly contributed to me becoming a hypochondriac. I was obsessed with finding something wrong with me because subconsciously I believed that I was supposed to die the day of the home invasion. I spent way too much time dwelling on all the things that had gone wrong that day and I hadn't spent nearly enough time being grateful for what had gone right and the grace that was in my life that allowed me to survive the whole ordeal in the first place. After 14 years of being held hostage by my fears, I decided to break free by reclaiming my focus, my mind and my time. I refused to spend another minute wrestling with what happened and decided to live the life that God had spared me with instead.

At some point healing began to take place in my life. I started to experience what felt like a purging. One day I felt like I woke up with a sense of newness. Something inside of me shifted. A fire was lit. I started to feel more like myself and I yearned for more feelings of freedom and emotional liberation.

## Introduction

I remember two different Pastors from two different parts of the world who prophesied to me and told me I was going to write a book. I remembered their words and the revelation thereof would play on my mind over and over keeping me awake at night. So, sleepless nights that used to be a result of pain-fueled insomnia turned into dreams and visions of healing, thoughts of possibilities and the transformative impact I could make in the lives of others as I laid awake.

The purpose fueled passion of writing this book brewed within me making me feel as though I was going to burst. I knew I had to get my message out. I thought about all the years I allowed fear to rob me and I wanted to help other men and women who may have found themselves living beneath their potential as a result of what they've been through. I had finally learned how to transcend my trauma and I wanted to help others do the same with their pain. God began placing people in my life who would pour into me like I had done for others even while dealing with my own pain.

God allowed me to live and I wanted to show him my appreciation by living a life of purpose, passion and impact. The day the intruder had a cocked and loaded automatic pistol to my head, I used my hands and my voice to lay hands on him and pray for him. My voice was heard in heaven. My prayer was heard and my hands were used as a vessel. I understand now why I was spared. Now when I have that vision of me laying in a pool of blood in my foyer, instead of it bringing me to tears, it now evokes praise. It was my pain that has given me power. I survived the attack so that I can now thrive on purpose.

I closed my personal clinic out of fear and went to work with my husband. I look at that as a set up. I gained more flexibility to be a mom, a wife and community partner. I'm free to help the community. I'm free to be me. It's all been a set up that has prepared me to make a great impact in the lives of others.

I wrote this book for men and women who like me, allowed trauma to put their lives on hold. I wrote this book to remind you that there is a recovery room within us.

I was running a successful practice while juggling the fragments of my brokenness. But God!

I want every person reading this book to know life and death truly lies in the power of the tongue.

Speak life. Speak over yourself. Speak over your business, your family and your friends.

It's ok to be bruised but know that you don't have to remain broken. It's ok to look in the mirror and see shattered pieces, just know that there is power to mend your brokenness. I too was once shattered, but I'm here today and I'm shining like never before. You may have survived the worst day of your life, but simply surviving is not enough. You deserve to thrive, to live, to love, to rest, to experience peace and to enjoy the luxury of comfort.

I know what it's like to be stripped of your sense of safety. I know what it's like to be at war with yourself trying to win the battle in your mind. I know what it's like to have your hopes and dreams delayed, not because you're not capable or worthy, but because fear has you paralyzed and in turn is sabotaging your potential.

As you turn each page, I pray that fear, anxiety, depression, worry, stress and the residue of trauma no longer take residence in your heart and mind. I hope that with each affirmation, shared lesson, and devotion allows you to break free of the shackles that bind you to things that no longer serve you, I pray that your slow dance with fear turns into a full-out break dance that liberates you from the bondage of your past. You deserve to live, love, learn and experience unspeakable joy. Get ready for your breakthrough. I declare that you are No Longer Trapped.

## Chapter One

# SLOW DANCING WITH FEAR

Fear according to Oxford dictionary is an unpleasant emotion caused by the belief that someone or something is dangerous, likely to cause pain or a threat. Fear can dwell in the mind and cause you to become a completely different person. After the home invasion, I became paralyzed mentally. I was still going about my day-to-day life, but I was living captive in my mind. Thoughts of someone hurting me had become consuming. My every waking thought was fear that someone wanted to kill me. I didn't share these feelings with anyone. Instead, I harbored them inside. I hid my relationship with fear from everyone around me. I forced myself to act as if I was fine whenever I was in the presence of others. I lied to myself for years trying to convince myself that I was over the robbery and the series of miscarriages. I would tell myself things like, "It wasn't that big of a deal!" or, "That was years ago!" It was all lies and white noise to deflect from the unrelenting pain I was carrying within. The truth of the matter was that \ I wasn't over anything. I was being strong for everyone around me so I wouldn't look weak or broken. However, I was living with the subconscious certainty that something or someone was going to harm me. It had become difficult for me to go to public functions. I had become a prisoner to my own thoughts. I recall being in a department store during the busy holiday shopping season. I was browsing around the shoe section when a group of shoppers got really close to me and I screamed in the store. It wasn't too loud, but it was loud enough to startle the people on the aisle with me.

I apologized to the onlookers as I came into the realization that I had my first panic attack at that moment. My heart was racing and I got extremely hot and sweaty in an instance. I hurriedly left the store but I sat in my car for about an hour before driving home. I replayed that moment over and over in my head ruminating the scenario continuously in private. I hid it from my family, friends and physicians. I didn't want it to be true. I didn't want to admit to anyone that I was afraid to live. My car became my safe space. I would often sit in my car to decompress. It provided me with all the privacy I wanted. I could cry, I could scream, and I could have my thoughts to myself. My car had become my secret place. It was my closet, my safe place and my sanctuary. As the panic attacks became more frequent, I began to learn my triggers. I learned to avoid certain movies, crowded rooms, closed spaces, and large events. At one point, I would feel like my thoughts were closing in on me. I couldn't breathe properly. It would trigger symptoms such as sweating, dizziness, chest pain, nausea, trembling and a fear of losing control. In most situations I would find the nearest exit and make it to a bathroom stall as soon as possible. I told no one! I always showed up with a smile so no one would suspect anything was wrong with me. To this day, I can not be in closed in spaces. I don't even like to use the restroom with the door closed, if I can help it. Fear did this to me. Imagine being too afraid to take a shower with the door closed because you must be able to hear the noises outside of the door. In my mind, if I can hear an imminent threat, I can brace for danger. This was the aftermath of the robbers kicking my door in, hearing the screams of my mother and three-year-old daughter and at the time, not being able to distinguish their screams from laughing or crying. As a result, my body wouldn't relax in confined spaces. From that day on, closed rooms have given me anxiety.

I can't even enjoy a movie in the theater room of my home because once the door closes, I can't hear what's happening on the outside of the door. My body stays in flight mode; always thinking of a way to escape. Think about that type of fear for a moment. It's paralyzing. Now think about living that way for years. Can you imagine? Fear does something to you that can be indescribable if you let it take over. It took over me, slowly. A daily slow dance. Fear forced me into solitude. I pushed a lot of my friends away and I backed away from a lot of people. It wasn't by choice. It was by design. Fear changed me. The way I viewed every relationship changed. I didn't fight for the relationships. I also didn't feel they fought to keep me. In my mind, I wondered how I was seen. This violent act against me shook me to my core, but yet I couldn't explain it to anyone. What if they knew the assailants? What if they really didn't care? Who do I talk to? I looked at everything through a pessimistic lens.

Fear alters your perception and will have you thinking everyone is your enemy.

The years following the home invasion robbery completely altered my brain chemistry and drastically changed the way I was able to experience the life I had built. In a sense, I had stopped living even though I was still alive. I looked happy to everyone on the outside looking in. I had a beautiful family, a successful business and some very sweet friends. I learned how to pretend and blend, I learned how to mask pain and I learned how to cry silently. I became a chameleon at living life by hiding my pain in plain sight. I was always scared that someone or something still wanted to kill me. I would often sit with myself and wonder, "How do I release this fear? How do I stop pretending I am ok? Why am I hiding? Why am I afraid for others to know what I'm struggling with internally? When did I become so consumed with what people thought about me? Who was I before the life changing incident? What type of life did

I live before my life changed?" This was the internal dialogue that plagued me. I didn't have any answers. I only had excuses. I had an excuse for everything only because I didn't want to face the reality that I needed help. I didn't want to acknowledge that I was broken.

How much can one bare?

Fear will affect every aspect of your life. Fear creeps in. It doesn't come on instantly. It's like a thief. It slowly robs you. It can be triggered by a loss of a job or a loved one, a tragic accident, a divorce, a car accident, or sometimes just because of our thoughts. That is when faith is needed.

Faith over fear is the motto I adopted to transcend the bondage of fear, pain and the aftermath of trauma. Faith according to the Oxford dictionary is defined as complete trust or confidence in someone or something. What or who is your something or someone? I had to ask myself this because I was at a point where either I was going to fight my fear with faith or slowly dance with it allowing it to kill parts of me with each step.

*Hebrews 11:1 states now faith is the substance of things hoped for and the evidence of things not seen.*

I couldn't see my way out, but I hoped and longed for it every waking moment. It boiled down to the fact that if I was ever going to be liberated from the anxiety induced state that had become my norm, I had to change my thoughts. When I started implementing a perspective of faith into my daily routine, it was hard at first. It was an hour-by-hour struggle. I would read positive affirmations daily and I would write love notes to myself on my phone. I knew I was loved by my husband and my family, but I needed to remind myself that I loved myself too. It was not my fault that any of these unfortunate events happened to me. Exercising faith can be difficult when you are in the thick of a fight with fear but you must be intentional about your healing. Faith is like a muscle; you must use it in order to strengthen it. I began each day with positive affirmations and meditation.

I began to believe my mind was healed. I would tell myself that I was healed. I had to combat every negative thought or doubt by immediately changing the narrative of my inner thoughts. My self-talk became a soul feeding dialogue that was fueled by faith. When you decide that you want to exist in a different state of mind, body and spirit your thoughts must be surrendered to God or your higher power daily. It will strengthen you. It takes deliberate action.The age old saying is true, " So, as a man thinks, so is he".

I challenge you to think new thoughts and to be bold enough to swap out ideas of fear with internal insight that brings you peace, joy and comfort. I know firsthand that this can be a very difficult shift when you've normalized existing in a state of fright, but what I know for sure is that it's possible to change, it's possible to heal and it's possible to reclaim your life. I spent 14 years slow dancing with fear and I'm writing this book as a declaration that at any moment you can choose to do a new dance. In fact, you deserve to dance with the freedom of feeling good in your body, peace in your mind and a sense of safety that comforts your soul. Happiness is a choice but joy is a gift. I desire for you to reclaim the type of joy into your life that is not moved by your circumstances. If you're like me and you've allowed the residue of trauma to deteriorate your quality of life, this is your sign that it's time to take back what the pain stole from you; It's never too late to think new thoughts. You can live again, you simply need to believe that you can.

CHAPTER TWO

# NAVIGATING SERIES OF LOSSES

*"Even though life sometimes brings on a series of losses, how you respond to those losses, what you make of what's left, and the perspective you hold as you process grief is what prepares you for what's next. Always believe in the beauty of what lies ahead."*
**~Dr. Shelita McGowan**

There are moments when I reflect on the many times when I was plagued with the devastation of loss, and the anticipation of more grief even in the face of things that were seemingly good. I had gotten to a point where I believed that losing was my nature and I didn't expect anything other than disappointment, bad news and more grief. During such dark moments in my life, it was hard to look forward to anything worthwhile because the series of losses that were showing up in my life took center stage. I was emotionally, spiritually and mentally bankrupt. I wanted so desperately to shake free from the pain of losing but every time I felt a glimpse of hope, recovery or healing, it was interrupted by yet another blow to my heart, mind, body & spirit. I wish I could tell you that in the face of loss I was yet hopeful. I wasn't. I was devastated, sad, angry, depressed, anxious and I had even developed a pessimistic perspective that was negatively impacting my marriage, my parenting, my work and even my ability to engage in and nurture relationships with friends, clients and colleagues. Truth is, I was stuck in a rut of inner turmoil, self-pity and a revolving door of grief. I couldn't understand why it was all happening to me. I was a good person with a good heart and that didn't shield me from experiencing good grief.

I never understood why the elders would consider grief "good". Nothing about losing felt good. Nothing about catastrophic change, or traumatic life disruption felt good. What I've come to discover after a series of hard losses, soul aching pain and ever flowing tears, is that it's not necessarily the grief within itself that is good. It is more so about who you become, the strength you embody and the emotional and spiritual fortitude you develop as a result of surviving loss and coming out better while yet still bruised afterwards. It's something about the inner strength required to alchemize pain into purpose, or to stand as a winner while still being wounded. There's a beauty to walking triumphantly after being consumed with debilitating trauma.

As I write this book, not only am I reminded of my own pain, but I stand here as a pillar of strength, and a living example that the pain you face today is positioning you for a greater tomorrow. I know it doesn't feel that way and I know it's probably the last thing you want to hear while you're nursing your fresh wounds. I know. I've been there; and while I can overstand the weight of dark seasons, hard losses, uncertainty and deep-rooted emotional injury, I now can testify to the good that I've reluctantly discovered as I've spent years slowly dancing with my fears and working through my grief. I can tell you that although now your heart may be heavy, in due season you too will receive wind beneath your wings to propel hope, love, joy and peace within you again. Your dreams will one day resurrect and the pain of today will become your inspired testimony for tomorrow. Surviving where you are right now and what you feel today will require that you believe that greater days ahead do exist; even if they feel so far away.

I was pregnant during the robbery that changed my life. I didn't know I was with child until I experienced a sudden miscarriage. A few months later, I was pregnant again when I was invited on the Dr. Phil Show to share my story of how trauma was impacting my life. While filming on set, my body initiated yet another spontaneous abortion causing me to lose another baby. After that, the miscarriages just kept happening. I experienced seven miscarriages in total before getting pregnant for the last time with twins. I ended up conceiving during the seventh pregnancy, but even then, I lost one of the twins which reaffirmed another loss in my life. Losing life after life forced me to come to terms with the truth that I was storing trauma in my womb. As a Chiropractic Physician, I understand the physiological effects of emotional injury and how it can manifest as physical pain and injuries. I realized that the miscarriages I was experiencing were a result of the disease I was still harboring internally. The stress of reliving my trauma was possibly creating a world of chaos in my womb that my babies couldn't survive in.

As a result of researching illnesses and symptoms of trauma, I became a hypochondriac. I kept thinking something was wrong with me although outside of trauma, I couldn't really pinpoint an exact cause. Prior to the robbery, I had none of these issues. If I came down with a cold, it was a cold. If I got a random bruise, it was just that... a bruise. After the robbery, a simple bruise was legitimate cause to consult google which led to a fearful assumption that perhaps the bruise was leukemia, a rare blood disorder or some other sort of life ending disease that I was doomed to have. Minor, yet common inconveniences turned into a deep plunge down a rabbit hole of stress; it was almost like an obsession. I started to do more research on the physical, mental and emotional aftermath of trauma. When the three armed men entered my home, my vagina was exposed. The violation of my privacy was hard to process, and while I believed at the time that I was working through it over the years. It was my body that was still keeping score of the inner turmoil that I was still toiling with.

Whenever I would go to the bathroom during any of my pregnancies, I would always look for blood. I would literally wipe with anticipation of seeing blood. I had gotten to a point where I was waiting to lose the baby because it was a pattern that I had grown to anticipate. I remember waking up one morning during one of my pregnancies and telling my husband that I wanted to get an ultrasound. I told him that I should call my doctor to see if she can give me an impromptu ultrasound. My husband quickly responded with some concern in his voice reminding me that it was Saturday and that it wasn't a common practice to simply request an ultrasound from your doctor and receive one the same day. However, when I woke up, I could sense that something was wrong. I called around and I found a facility that could get me in for an ultrasound. Their office had a cancellation and they were able to get me in.

She performed the ultrasound and just like I had suspected, her face assured me of what I had already expected. She encouraged me to go to the emergency room and to follow up with my doctor right away because she was unable to detect a heartbeat. She paused and said, "I need you to go to the hospital right now." I was crushed but not surprised, heartbroken but somewhat numb to the news. The majority of my miscarriages happened right after the first trimester. The longest I carried a baby before a miscarriage had been 17 weeks. He was a boy. After that particular miscarriage, I had a D&C. His body was sent off and according to medical records he passed away in the womb due to Trisomy 13.

One of the most challenging nuances was facing family, friends, colleagues, and my church community after each loss. They would ask, "are you pregnant again" or make statements like "oh you lost another baby" their comments became more painful than the actual loss at times. The fact that they noticed what was happening, forced me to feel it and I preferred being numb. When I was pregnant for the seventh time with twins, I started bleeding spontaneously. I went to the emergency room. The physicians informed me that I was in fact miscarrying again, although one of the babies was doing very well in his sac.

I was so used to losing, but it was something about the seventh pregnancy that allowed me to see a glimpse of hope, even in what was still a very hard place. Even though I was experiencing another loss, God showed me promise in the midst of it all.

Over the course of 14 years I suffered 7 miscarriages. I had become so used to loss that I started anticipating it, but it was something about the last miscarriage that shifted everything for me. While I was losing one fetus, the other was safe in his sac. After successfully giving birth to my son, a new found sense of hope emerged. I realized that even after a series of losses, God could restore you in a time that feels like you are still losing. I received hope and healing while I was emotionally in a hard place. It was the beauty of new beginnings bestowed upon me during the birth of my son that reestablished a sense of goodness in my life. I'm reminded of a scripture that gave me comfort during that time in my life; 2 Corinthians 12:9, "He said to me, "My grace is sufficient for you, for my power is made perfect in weakness." I experienced the grace of God in action during my seventh miscarriage. It reminded me that at any given moment, your life can change for the better. It forced me to center my thoughts on hope and the possibility of blessings even after a series of losses. What I want you to know is that while life may bring us face to face with loss, pain and grief; these hard and heavy instances don't have to be the final chapter. Life goes on after loss if you choose to hang on to faith and cling to hope. Sometimes it may feel like you're hanging on to hope by a thread but hang on anyway.

*1 Peter 5:10 " After you have suffered a little while, the God of all grace, who has called you to his eternal glory in Christ, will himself restore, confirm, strengthen and establish you"*

Anticipatory grief is often referred to as anticipatory loss or preparatory grief; it is the distress a person may feel in the days, months or even years before the death of a loved one or other impending loss. Anticipatory grief keeps you in a state of grieving long before loss occurs. If we're not careful we can get stuck in this state of despair. I spent so much time expecting things to go wrong that I lost hope for things to go right until that fateful day when things were going right and wrong at the same time. This moment of duality shifted my perspective and allowed me to see that contrary to what I had come to expect; good things were still possible and that I didn't have to only make room for grief, I could hold space for goodness.

I want you to take some time to offer up space for good things to happen to you and for you. Instead of anticipating grief, I want you to practice the expectation of goodness, abundance and the flow of grace into your life. This may require you to step outside of your comfort zone and it may feel foreign and even scary at first. But I want you to start thinking about life through the lens of goodness and hope. If you weren't consumed with the pain of yesterday, what would you hope for? What dreams would you pursue? How would you show up differently for yourself? Would you wear the nice dress you've allowed to sit in the back of your closet until a "good day" warranted you to wear it? When was the last time you laughed without fear of the future? When was the last time you allowed yourself to be present and in the moment?

Affirm to yourself that you are safe in your body, you are protected and you are both worthy and deserving of experiencing all the good that life has to offer and then take some time to reflect and write out what a life free of fear would look and feel like for you. List out possible best case scenarios in your life instead of allowing worst case scenarios to dominate your life.

_____

_____

_____

_____

_____

_____

_____

_____

_____

_____

_____

_____

_____

# NO LONGER TRAPPED

## Chapter Three

# NEW HEALING FOR OLD WOUNDS EMBRACING HEALING AND FINDING FREEDOM

*"Healing is an art. It takes practice, it takes time, it takes patience and it takes love."*
**-Maza Dohta**

From the depths of my own experiences, I have learned that healing is not a passive process—it requires intention, courage, and a relentless pursuit of freedom. In the pages of "No Longer Trapped," I share my journey, the trials I endured, and the invaluable lessons I learned along the way. Today, I invite you to join me on this transformative path as we explore the profound significance of embracing healing and finding freedom.

One of the biggest lessons I learned on my journey of triumphing over trauma was the personal responsibility we must take over our healing even when we weren't responsible for the things that traumatized us in the first place.

We must take an active role in our journey to wholeness. It is about recognizing that we have the power to reshape our thoughts, to refocus our minds, and to redirect our paths. This self-awareness is crucial, for no matter how much support we receive, we must genuinely take ownership over our feelings and actively seek our own well-being.

Recalibrating our minds becomes paramount in this process. We learn to identify thoughts that serve us and those that do not. It is like discerning between a road that leads to growth and a path that only leads to more pain. Developing the ability to recognize these thoughts and having an instant self-care fix—a mechanism to refocus and ground ourselves—is instrumental. Trust me; even I am still learning this delicate art of self-redirection. But it is a skill that empowers us to take control, as the scriptures say, and take captive the thoughts that threaten to engulf us.

I want you to know that your journey does not end with the trauma you have experienced. This is not the end of your story; it is merely a chapter that can become a turning point. The pain, the fear, the anxiety—they may all try to take hold of you, but they do not define you. You are so much more than your past. By allowing yourself to go through the necessary steps—grieving, acknowledging anger, confronting fear—you can release the hold they have on you. Understand that healing is not an instant process. It is a journey that unfolds over time, with its own stages of grief and emotional complexities.

Let me emphasize this: you are not expected to suppress your pain or make it disappear. That would be an unrealistic expectation. There is no shame in acknowledging your hurt, in sharing what you have been through. Do not be embarrassed or afraid to voice your story. Sometimes, we tend to keep our traumas hidden, fearing judgment or dismissal. But it is within these narratives that healing finds its roots. It is in the vulnerability of sharing that we create a space for understanding, empathy, and growth.

Finding an outlet becomes paramount—an outlet where you can safely express yourself, unravel your emotions, and unload the burdens that weigh you down. This outlet can take many forms—a trusted friend, a journal, or a professional counselor. But it must be someone or something that allows you to unfold completely, without judgment or condemnation. Compartmentalizing your pain only adds to the hurt, leaving unresolved wounds that may resurface when triggered by new experiences.

Undoubtedly, triggers will arise along your healing journey. They can be unpredictable and overwhelming, sometimes leaving you wondering why you are still affected by certain things.

Life is a tapestry of experiences, emotions, and interactions that shape our reality. Sometimes, seemingly insignificant events can trigger a storm of emotions within us, leading to inner chaos and unrest. These triggers, rooted in our past experiences and beliefs, can disrupt our peace and hinder our personal growth. When you learn to identify your triggers, you can unravel their origins, and empower yourself to navigate through life with greater self-awareness and inner harmony.

**Understanding Triggers:**
1. Triggers are external stimuli or internal thoughts that evoke intense emotional reactions within us. They can vary from person to person and may be rooted in

past traumas, unresolved conflicts, or deeply ingrained beliefs. By understanding triggers, we can gain insight into our emotional landscape and develop the tools to respond rather than react.

**Cultivating Self-Awareness:**

2. Self-awareness is the key to identifying triggers and their impact on our well-being. Cultivate a practice of mindfulness and introspection to observe your thoughts, emotions, and bodily sensations without judgment. Pay attention to patterns that arise during certain situations or interactions. Notice when you feel an emotional shift or when old wounds resurface. This self-awareness is the foundation for healing and growth.

**Unraveling the Origins:**

3. To effectively manage triggers, it's essential to explore their origins. Take the time to reflect on past experiences, traumas, and belief systems that may

have contributed to their formation. Engage in journaling, therapy, or discussions with trusted individuals to gain deeper insights. By unraveling the origins of triggers, you can begin to heal the wounds and rewrite the narratives that no longer serve you.

**Creating a Trigger Map:**
4. Creating a trigger map can be a powerful tool for understanding and navigating your triggers. List the common situations, people, or thoughts that tend to trigger intense emotional responses within you. Reflect on the emotions associated with each trigger and the underlying beliefs that may be contributing to them. This visual representation will help you gain clarity and identify potential areas for growth and healing.

**Developing Coping Strategies:**
5. Once you have identified your triggers, it's crucial to develop healthy coping strategies. Explore self-

soothing techniques such as deep breathing exercises, mindfulness practices, or engaging in activities that bring you joy and relaxation. Consider seeking professional support or joining support groups to learn additional coping mechanisms from others who have similar experiences. These strategies will empower you to respond to triggers in a constructive and compassionate manner.

**Embracing Self-Care:**

6. Self-care is a fundamental aspect of managing triggers and maintaining inner harmony. Prioritize activities that nurture your physical, emotional, and mental well-being. Engage in regular exercise, practice self-compassion, maintain healthy boundaries, and surround yourself with a supportive network of individuals who understand and respect your journey. Self-care acts as a shield, helping you

navigate through triggering situations with resilience and grace.

Learning to identify and manage triggers is a transformative journey toward self-empowerment and inner peace. By cultivating self-awareness, unraveling their origins, and implementing effective coping strategies, you can navigate through life with greater ease and harmony. Embrace this process with patience and compassion, as triggers are opportunities for growth and healing. Remember, you have the power to rewrite your narrative and reclaim your emotional well-being. Embrace the journey of self-discovery, and let the unraveling of triggers be the gateway to a life filled with serenity and personal transformation.

_____

_____

_____

_____

_____

# NO LONGER TRAPPED

## Chapter Four

# RECLAIMING PEACE, PURPOSE AND PERSONAL POWER

*"You will find peace not by trying to escape your problems, but by confronting them courageously. You will find peace not in denial, but in victory."*
**- J. Donald Walters**

The journey towards reclaiming peace, purpose, and personal power begins with acknowledging the impact of the trauma on your life. For years, I carried the weight of my past, feeling trapped and powerless. I had lost touch with the essence of who I was and what I truly desired in life. But deep within me, a flicker of hope remained, urging me to embark on a path of healing and self-discovery.

The first step I took was to seek support. I reached out to trusted friends, family, and professionals who could provide a safe space for me to heal. Through therapy, I began unraveling the layers of pain and fear that had consumed me for far too long. It was not an easy journey, but with each session, I gained a deeper understanding of my trauma and its impact on my life.

Reclaiming peace meant finding inner calm amidst the chaos. I discovered the power of mindfulness and prayerful practices that allowed me to connect with the present moment in order to cultivate a sense of tranquility within. By embracing self-care and self-compassion, I learned to soothe my wounded soul and nurture myself back to wholeness. Through these practices, I reclaimed a sense of peace that had eluded me for years.

Finding purpose was a transformative experience. I rediscovered what truly brought me joy and fulfillment. I realized that my trauma had given me a unique perspective and a burning desire to help others on their own healing journeys. I stepped outside of fear, sought out support and immersed myself into trauma recovery. By aligning my life with my purpose, I found a renewed sense of meaning and direction.

But perhaps the most empowering aspect of my journey was reclaiming my personal power. I had allowed the trauma to define me and dictate my choices long enough and it was time to take back control of my life. I embarked on a path of self-empowerment, embracing my strengths and rediscovering my worth. I set boundaries, both with others and with myself, honoring my needs and desires. I surrounded myself with a supportive community that uplifted and encouraged me along the way.

Reclaiming peace, purpose, and personal power has brought countless benefits into my life. It has allowed me to cultivate deep and meaningful relationships built on trust and authenticity. It has given me the courage to pursue my dreams and make a positive impact in the world. It has granted me the freedom to live life on my own terms, free from the shackles of past traumas.

These three elements - peace, purpose, and personal power - are vital for a fulfilling and meaningful life. Peace brings inner harmony and a sense of well-being. Purpose infuses our existence with meaning and drives us to make a difference. Personal power empowers us to take control of our lives and create the future we desire.

If you find yourself on a similar journey of healing and transformation, I encourage you to believe in your own resilience and capacity for growth. Seek support, embrace self-care, self-compassion, and explore your passions. Set boundaries, honor your needs, and surround yourself with a supportive community.

The journey to reclaiming peace, purpose, and personal power is a transformative one. It requires courage, vulnerability, and a deep commitment to healing, but the rewards are immeasurable. As you embark on this journey, remember that you are not alone. There are countless others who have walked this path before you and are now living vibrant and fulfilling lives. You have the power within you to heal, to thrive, and to reclaim your life. Embrace it with open arms, and let the light of your true self shine brightly once again.

## The Benefits of Reclaiming Peace, Purpose, and Personal Power

Before diving into the practical steps of reclaiming peace, purpose, and personal power, it is essential to understand the tremendous benefits they bring to our lives. When we embark on this journey, we unlock the following transformative gifts:

1. Inner Harmony and Serenity: Reclaiming peace allows us to silence the chaotic noise within and cultivate a deep sense of inner calm. It enables us to heal emotional wounds, find solace in the present moment, and restore balance to our lives. With inner harmony, we can navigate life's challenges with resilience and grace.

2. Meaning and Fulfillment: Purpose breathes life into our existence. It ignites a fire within, propelling us forward with clarity, motivation, and a sense of direction. Reconnecting with our purpose after trauma provides a renewed sense of meaning and fulfillment, guiding us towards a life aligned with our values and passions.

3. Empowerment and Self-Agency: Personal power is the innate strength we possess to shape our lives and make choices that align with our authentic selves. Reclaiming personal power after trauma restores our

belief in our capabilities, helps us establish healthy boundaries, and empowers us to live life on our own terms.

Take a moment to envision the life you desire, one filled with peace, purpose, and personal power. In your journal, reflect on the following questions:

1. Peace: What does peace look and feel like to you? How has trauma impacted your sense of inner peace? What actions can you take today, no matter how small, to cultivate peace within yourself and in your daily life?

2. Purpose: What gives your life meaning and purpose? How has trauma affected your sense of purpose? Consider your passions, values, and strengths. How can you align your actions with your purpose? What steps can you take to reconnect with or discover new aspects of your purpose?

3. Personal Power: How has trauma affected your sense of personal power and agency? What does personal power mean to you? In what areas of your life do you want to reclaim your power? Identify specific actions or behaviors that will help you regain a sense of control, autonomy, and confidence.

Now, take a moment to reflect on the insights you've gained. What small, actionable steps can you commit to taking to begin reclaiming peace, purpose, and personal power in your life? Write down at least three actions you can start implementing immediately.

Remember, this is a personal journey, and progress may come in small steps. Be gentle with yourself and celebrate even the smallest victories along the way. Use this journaling practice as a tool for self-discovery, self-compassion, and taking inspired action towards reclaiming the life you deserve.

# Reclaiming Peace, Purpose and Personal Power

# NO LONGER TRAPPED

Chapter Five

# "THE TEST OF TRUSTING AGAIN"

*"Be bold enough to trust yourself, you have survived a lot, and you will survive whatever is coming. You are brilliantly resilient and intrinsically aware of what you need to recover, heal, transform and thrive"*

One of the pivotal moments in my journey was learning to trust again. Trust is an essential component of healthy relationships, whether they be personal or professional. However, when we experience trauma, it can shatter our ability to trust ourselves, others, and the world around us. It becomes a constant battle between fear and vulnerability.

To begin the process of rebuilding trust, I had to remind myself that not everything that happened was my fault. I needed to release the weight of responsibility that I carried for the actions of others. It was crucial to stop assuming the worst in people and looking for loopholes in their stories. By doing so, I was hindering myself from forming genuine connections and living fully in the present moment.

Reclaiming your peace requires a shift in perspective. Trauma and distrust can shatter our outlook on life, but it doesn't have to define our future. It's essential to hold onto hope and recognize that one negative experience doesn't invalidate all the positive moments and opportunities that await us.

To those who find themselves in the dark, feeling isolated and impacted by distrust, I encourage you to take the first step towards freedom. Acknowledge your fear and recognize that self-preservation should not equate to isolation. Choose to change the way you look at life,

"The Test of Trusting Again"

despite the challenges you've faced. Remember that there are countless good things that can and will happen in your life.

Stepping out of isolation requires courage and self-trust. I vividly remember feeling lonely, yet realizing that it was by choice. I had people around me whom I could connect with, but I was hesitant to open myself up to them. I added loneliness to my fears, which only exacerbated the situation. It was a pivotal moment when I recognized that I had control over the company I kept and how close I allowed people to get to me.

To those seeking freedom from isolation, I urge you to take that first step. Don't be afraid to open your mouth and talk, to meet new people, regardless of your age or circumstances. God places individuals in our lives for various reasons and seasons. Trust the process and have faith that the right people will come into your life at the right time.

Learning to trust again begins with trusting yourself. Understand that you have the power to make the right decisions and that you deserve love and connection. It's important to give yourself the space to make mistakes, to grow, and to forgive yourself along the way.

While it is crucial to exercise caution and discernment, don't let the fear of being hurt again prevent you from trusting others. Embrace vulnerability, both in giving and receiving it. Remember, not everyone will be worthy of your trust, but gradually, you will find individuals who demonstrate their trustworthiness over time.

Reclaiming your peace and embracing the promises attached to your life is a journey that requires self-reflection, trust, and a shift in perspective. Release the burdens of the past and choose to focus on the possibilities of the future. Be courageous and step out of isolation, knowing that you have the power to control your company and the connections you make.

"The Test of Trusting Again"

Trust yourself, trust the process, and trust that there are genuine, trustworthy people out there waiting to walk this journey with you. Reclaim your peace, embrace the promises of life, and remember that healing and connection are within your reach.

I want you to begin to take the necessary steps to reestablishing trust within yourself and others. It can be a daunting task but it is necessary in order to rebuild healthy relationship dynamics.

1. Acknowledge the Impact: Recognize and acknowledge the trauma you have experienced, understanding its effects on your ability to trust yourself and others. This step involves validating your emotions and giving yourself permission to heal.

2. Seek Professional Support: Consider seeking support from a therapist or counselor experienced in trauma therapy. They can provide guidance, tools, and

techniques to help you navigate the healing process and rebuild trust.

3. Practice Self-Compassion: Be kind and patient with yourself throughout the healing journey. Practice self-compassion by forgiving yourself for any perceived mistakes or shortcomings. Remind yourself that healing takes time and progress is not always linear.

4. Engage in Self-Reflection: Take time to reflect on your values, boundaries, and personal needs. Understand what you require in relationships to feel safe and secure. This self-awareness will guide you in establishing healthy boundaries and making informed choices.

5. Start Small: Begin rebuilding trust with small, manageable steps. This might involve opening up to a trusted friend or family member about your feelings, sharing your experiences in a support

group, or participating in activities that bring you joy and a sense of connection.

6. Set Realistic Expectations: Recognize that rebuilding trust is a gradual process. Set realistic expectations for yourself and others, understanding that trust is earned over time. Allow yourself to take it one step at a time, celebrating each milestone along the way.

7. Communicate Openly: Foster open and honest communication with yourself and others. Express your thoughts, feelings, and concerns in a respectful manner. Clear and transparent communication can help establish a foundation of trust and deepen connections.

8. Prioritize Boundaries: Establish clear boundaries that protect your physical, emotional, and mental well-being. Communicate these boundaries effectively and assertively. Respecting your boundaries allows you to regain a sense of control and security.

9. Practice Forgiveness: Consider forgiveness as a means of letting go of resentment and pain. This doesn't mean forgetting or condoning the actions that caused the trauma, but rather freeing yourself from the burden of holding onto negative emotions. Forgiveness can be a powerful step towards healing and rebuilding trust.

10. Surround Yourself with Supportive People: Surround yourself with a supportive network of individuals who genuinely care for your well-being. Build relationships with people who demonstrate trustworthiness, empathy, and respect. These positive connections will reinforce your belief in the possibility of trustworthy relationships.

Remember, healing from trauma and rebuilding trust is a personal journey that takes time and self-compassion. Each step you take, no matter how small, brings you closer to reclaiming your trust in yourself and others.

Reflect on a specific incident or experience that has impacted your ability to trust yourself and others. Write about the following:

1. Description: Provide a detailed description of the incident or experience that shattered your trust. What happened? How did it make you feel? How did it affect your relationships and your perception of yourself?

2. Impact: Explore the ways in which this incident or experience has influenced your trust in yourself and others. How has it affected your ability to trust your own judgment, instincts, or decisions? How has it affected your willingness to trust others?

3. Self-Reflection: Take a moment to reflect on your personal values, boundaries, and needs in relationships. How have these been affected by the

incident? Are there any patterns or beliefs that you have developed as a result of the trauma? How do these patterns or beliefs impact your ability to trust?

4. Rebuilding Trust: Identify three small steps you can take to begin rebuilding trust within yourself and others. These steps should be specific and actionable. For example, it could be opening up to a trusted friend about your feelings, practicing self-compassion daily, or setting clear boundaries in your relationships.

5. Support System: Reflect on the importance of having a support system during the healing process. Consider who in your life can provide support, understanding, and encouragement as you work towards rebuilding trust. How can you seek their support or communicate your needs to them?

6. Self-Compassion: Explore the concept of self-compassion and its role in rebuilding trust. How can

you cultivate self-compassion in your life? What self-compassionate practices or affirmations can you incorporate into your daily routine to nurture yourself during this healing journey?

7. Vision for the Future: Envision a future where you have rebuilt trust within yourself and others. How does it look and feel? What positive changes do you anticipate in your relationships, self-esteem, and overall well-being? Describe this vision in detail and let it inspire and motivate you.

Remember, journaling is a personal and introspective process. Take your time, be honest with yourself, and allow your thoughts and emotions to flow freely. Use this journal prompt as a starting point to explore your experiences, nurture self-reflection, and pave the way towards rebuilding trust within yourself and others.

## Chapter Six

# "DO A NEW DANCE" DESIGNING A NEW VISION FOR YOUR LIFE

*"A well designed life is a life that is generative-
it is constantly changing, evolving
and it is always a possibility for newness to
emerge if you allow yourself to design a new
vision for your life"*

Slow dancing with fear is a powerful metaphor for the intimate time I spent nursing and rehearsing my pain and my fears. Reaching the end of my daunting dance meant embarking on a new one- a dance filled with faith, realigned dreams, hope and fearlessness.

In order to design a new vision for my life, I would first have to metaphorically do a new dance. I had to stop bringing my worry to the dance floor, and instead invite purpose to join me in a brand new two-step. My healing journey was not only transformative, but it was resounding in the sense that it allowed me to understand the divine duality of both pain and purpose. Most people avoid the hard conversations and heavy feelings that precede healing but sometimes the only way over hard things is to work through them. The work required is as unique as the experiences that require our healing in the first place. Your healing journey is sacred and it will mirror your limitations and pain points so that restoration can begin within you.

No matter where you are in your journey, give yourself permission to grant yourself grace throughout the process. When it was brought to my attention from my physician that she suspected that I was clinically depressed, denial was my initial response. I was so used to pushing the trauma aside and pretending it hadn't affected me, but having someone whom I respected confront the idea forced me to take a deeper look within. I eventually came to accept that I was in fact living with clinical depression, but then came anger. It was like a quietly brewing rage triggered by the smallest of things, leaving me bewildered by the intensity of my reactions. Through therapy, I gradually uncovered layers of my healing process. Tears flowed as I recounted the moment when the weight of my depression became a reality. I realized that even my subsequent crying spells were intertwined with my acceptance of being clinically depressed. Anxiety emerged, intensifying my experiences. I felt constantly on edge, startled by the simplest of things, and my heart raced, making it difficult to breathe and think clearly. Depression and anxiety often overlapped, causing an emotional roller coaster ride where I couldn't predict what season I would find myself in.

The non-linear nature of the healing process became apparent to me. There was no set order or timeframe for each stage. It wasn't a neat progression from depression to stress to anxiety. Instead, it was a tangled web of emotions, with different stages resurfacing at unexpected times. I couldn't predict when the depression would slowly creep back in, questioning how it managed to find its way back into my life. I began to understand that unaddressed trauma could resurface even years later, impacting my emotional well-being without my conscious awareness.

So, how would I know when I had crossed over to the other side, when I could change my dance from the slow waltz with fear to the vibrant tango with my dreams and joy? For me, it was a feeling that accompanied the act of sharing my story. In the past, discussing the trauma had brought shame, judgment, anxiety, stress, and depression. But now, I find myself able to talk about it without tears, without feeling the weight of judgment upon me. I can speak freely and acknowledge what has happened to me.

I realized that healing was not about erasing the past or forgetting what had transpired. It was about reaching a point where I could discuss my experiences without being consumed by negative emotions. It meant finding freedom and releasing the shame that had clung to me for so long. And as I embarked on this new dance, I knew it was time to let go of the cycle of fear, depression, anxiety, and stress. It was time to actively choose happiness, to take small steps each day towards joy, and to prioritize my own well-being.

There may never be a definitive end to the healing process, but I knew that by consciously deciding to dance with faith, dreams, hope, and fearlessness, I was stepping into a new chapter of my life. I wanted to share this newfound perspective with others and provide them with the tools and insights to navigate their own healing journeys. Together, we could embrace the complexities, face our fears, and find solace in the knowledge that we were not alone. We could learn to dance again, this time with our heads held high and our hearts open to the beauty and possibilities life had to offer.

It's important for you to understand the five stages of grief that often accompany trauma based experiences. Recognize what stage you may be in and then decide to embark on the steps necessary to embrace healing

1. **Denial:**
   - Acknowledge the denial stage as a natural defense mechanism.
   - Seek support from loved ones or professionals who can gently help you confront the reality of the situation.
   - Engage in self-reflection and explore the underlying emotions behind the denial.
   - Practice acceptance and gradually let go of resistance to the truth.

## 2. Anger:

- Allow yourself to feel and express your anger in a healthy way, such as through journaling, exercise, or talking to a trusted friend.
- Engage in activities that help release pent-up emotions, such as art therapy or physical exercise.
- Practice self-compassion and forgiveness, both towards yourself and others involved.
- Consider seeking professional therapy or counseling to process and manage anger effectively.

## 3. Bargaining:

- Recognize that bargaining is a way of trying to regain control or find a sense of hope.
- Practice self-reflection to understand the underlying needs or fears driving the bargaining stage.

- Seek support from a therapist or counselor to explore healthier coping mechanisms and develop realistic expectations.
- Focus on self-care and engage in activities that promote self-empowerment and self-acceptance.

## 4. Depression:

- Allow yourself to grieve and mourn the losses associated with the trauma or grief.
- Reach out to a support network of friends, family, or support groups who can provide empathy and understanding.
- Consider therapy or counseling to address underlying emotional issues and develop coping strategies for managing depression.
- Engage in self-care activities that promote emotional well-being, such as practicing mindfulness, engaging in hobbies, or seeking solace in nature.

**5. Acceptance:**

- Understand that acceptance does not mean forgetting or minimizing the trauma or grief but rather finding a way to integrate it into your life.

- Continue therapy or counseling to maintain emotional well-being and address any residual issues.

- Engage in self-reflection and personal growth activities to find meaning and purpose beyond the trauma or grief.

- Seek support from others who have experienced similar challenges, such as joining support groups or online communities.

Remember, healing is a unique and personal journey. It is important to be patient and gentle with yourself as you navigate through the stages of grief and trauma. Seeking professional help is highly recommended to provide tailored guidance and support throughout the healing process.

Life has a way of throwing unexpected challenges our way, leaving us feeling lost, broken, and uncertain about the future. Trauma can have a profound impact on our lives, shaking the very foundations of who we are and what we believe in. But amidst the pain and chaos, there lies an opportunity for transformation. This chapter aims to inspire and guide you as you embark on the journey of designing a new vision for your life after healing from trauma. It's time to reclaim your power, redefine your purpose, and create a life that is authentically yours.

**Reflect on Your Journey:**
1. Take a moment to acknowledge the tremendous strength and resilience you have demonstrated in your healing process. Reflect on the lessons learned, the growth you have experienced, and the strengths

you have discovered within yourself. Recognize that your past does not define you, but rather serves as a stepping stone towards a brighter future.

**Rediscover Your Passions and Purpose:**

2. Reconnecting with your passions and purpose is a powerful way to design a new vision for your life. Explore activities that ignite your soul, make you feel alive, and bring joy and fulfillment. Reflect on your values, dreams, and aspirations. What truly matters to you? What legacy do you want to leave behind? Allow yourself to dream without limitations and envision a life aligned with your deepest desires.

**Set Clear Goals and Intentions:**

3. Once you have identified your passions and purpose, it's time to set clear goals and intentions. Break down your vision into actionable steps that will propel you forward. Create a roadmap outlining short-term and long-term goals, ensuring they are specific,

measurable, achievable, relevant, and time-bound (SMART). Remember that progress is more important than perfection, so celebrate each step you take towards your new life.

**Cultivate a Supportive Network:**
4. Surround yourself with a supportive network of individuals who uplift, encourage, and inspire you. Seek out mentors, coaches, or therapists who can guide you through your journey of self-discovery and personal growth. Connect with like-minded individuals who share similar aspirations, joining communities or groups that foster positivity and collaboration. Together, you can create a strong foundation for building your new life.

**Embrace Self-Care and Well-being:**
5. Nurturing your well-being is essential as you design your new life. Prioritize self-care and incorporate practices that nourish your mind, body, and soul.

Practice mindfulness, engage in regular physical exercise, adopt a balanced diet, and ensure you get enough rest and relaxation. Take time for self-reflection, journaling, or meditation to foster inner clarity and cultivate a positive mindset.

**Embrace Resilience and Adaptability:**

6. Life is unpredictable, and setbacks may occur along your journey. Embrace resilience and adaptability as essential skills to navigate through challenges. Embrace the mindset that every obstacle is an opportunity for growth and learning. When faced with adversity, tap into your inner strength, reevaluate your goals if necessary, and adjust your course while staying true to your vision.

Designing a new vision for your life after healing from trauma is a testament to your resilience and courage. It is an opportunity to rediscover who you truly are, to rewrite your story, and to create a life that aligns with your authentic self. Remember that this journey is unique to you, and it may take time and patience. Embrace the process, trust in your own abilities, and never underestimate the power within you. Your new life is waiting to be designed, so take the first step today and embark on this transformative adventure of self-discovery.

_____

_____

_____

_____

_____

_____

_____

_____

_____

_____

_____

_____

## Chapter Seven

# DARING TO
# DO A NEW DANCE

As I reflect on the process of stepping into the sheer boldness to recover from life altering emotional injury and mental anguish, I am reminded of the profound resilience and unwavering spirit within us all. It is a testament to the strength of the human soul, the power of therapy, the transformative nature of perspective shifts, and the courage to confront the shadows that can hold us captive if we don't fight to redeem peace after we have endured great pain.

In the beginning, fear was my constant companion, suffocating my dreams and casting a shadow over every aspect of my life. Its grip was tight, its whispers deafening, and I found myself locked in a slow dance that seemed to have no end. But through sheer determination and the support of incredible individuals who believed in my potential, I embarked on a journey of healing that has forever changed the course of my life.

Therapy became the sanctuary where I unraveled the tangled threads of my past, bravely facing the pain and allowing myself to feel it in its entirety. It was within those safe spaces that I discovered the transformative power of vulnerability, of sharing my deepest wounds and darkest fears with a compassionate guide who held space for my healing.

Through therapy, I learned to shift my perspective, unveiling the limiting beliefs that had held me captive for far too long. I rewrote my narrative, replacing self-doubt with self-compassion and fear with courage. The process was not linear; it demanded patience, resilience, and countless moments of self-reflection. But with each step forward, I discovered an untapped wellspring of strength that I never knew existed.

Today, as I stand on the other side of my pain, I no longer slow dance with fear and I am no longer trapped by the pain of my past. I have embraced a new rhythm, a dance of liberation, where I am fully present in each moment, unafraid to embrace the beauty and uncertainty of life. The shackles that once bound me have been shattered, and in their place, I have found freedom and joy.

This newfound liberation has ignited a fire within me, compelling me to encourage others to step onto the dance floor of their dreams. I want to share with the world the transformative power of healing, the strength that lies within vulnerability, and the unwavering courage that resides in each one of us. I have come to understand that fear is not our enemy, but rather a catalyst for growth and an invitation to be bold and courageous enough to embrace change, adjust to disruption and transcend trauma with the determination to heal.

So, as you reach the end of this book, I invite you to reflect on your own relationship with fear. Are you ready to release the bondage it holds over you? Can you feel the rhythm of your dreams pulsating within your heart? Embrace the therapeutic process of recovery, submit to the perspective shifts, and tap into the courage that dwells within you. Trust that you have the power to rewrite your narrative and create a life that is uniquely yours.

Dance with your dreams. Allow the music of your soul to guide your steps, and with every twirl and every leap, release yourself from the bondage of fear. Embrace the freedom that awaits you on the other side. Create a world where liberation is not just a dream, but a reality that is awakened when you dare to be bold and courageous enough to step onto the dance floor of your life.

May my story be an inspiring testament to the resilience of the human spirit, and a reminder that within each of us lies the power to heal, transform, and dance with the boundless joy of living intentionally, focusing on purpose, resting in gratitude and rejoicing that as we heal our hearts and minds, we are *No Longer Trapped.*

---
---
---
---
---
---
---
---
---
---
---
---

## NO LONGER TRAPPED

# NO LONGER TRAPPED
## DAILY AFFIRMATIONS

I release all fear and embrace the boundless possibilities that await me.

Each day, I am healing and growing stronger, both physically and emotionally.

I am deserving of love, joy, and all the good that life has to offer.

My past does not define me; I am creating a new and empowered future.

I choose to let go of what no longer serves me and make space for positive change.

I am resilient, and I have the strength to overcome any challenge that comes my way.

Every step I take brings me closer to healing and wholeness.

I trust in the process of healing and allow it to unfold naturally.

I release the pain of the past and open myself to receive deep inner peace.

I am worthy of happiness, and I choose to embrace it fully.

Fear does not control me; I am in charge of my thoughts and emotions.

I release the need for approval from others and validate myself from within.

I am surrounded by love and support, and I attract positive and uplifting relationships.

I am guided by my inner wisdom and intuition in making choices that align with my purpose.

I forgive myself and others, releasing any resentment or bitterness that hinders my growth.

I am grateful for the lessons I have learned from my past, as they have shaped me into who I am today.

I am a beacon of light, inspiring others with my courage and resilience.

I choose to see challenges as opportunities for growth and transformation.

I embrace my unique talents and gifts, sharing them with the world in a way that brings me joy and fulfillment.

I am connected to a higher purpose, and I trust in the divine plan for my life.

Each day, I step into my power, living authentically and fearlessly, knowing that I am on the path to living a purposeful and fulfilling life.

I release all limiting beliefs and embrace the limitless potential within me.

I am worthy of all the abundance and success that comes my way.

I am deserving of deep love, compassion, and understanding.

I am a magnet for positive experiences and attract positivity into my life.

I trust in God's plan for me and surrender to His guidance.

I am surrounded by a supportive and nurturing community that uplifts and inspires me.

I release the need to compare myself to others and fully embrace my unique journey.

I am an embodiment of love and radiate love in all that I do.

# No Longer Trapped Daily Affirmations

I release the need to control outcomes and trust in the natural flow of life.

I am the author of my own story, and I choose to create a narrative filled with joy, resilience, and triumph.

I acknowledge my inner strength and tap into it whenever faced with challenges.

I release any attachments to past traumas and embrace the present moment with open arms.

I am open to receiving healing and I allow it to restore balance and harmony within me.

I am a catalyst for positive change, making a difference in the world through my actions and words.

I honor my emotions and give myself permission to feel and express them authentically.

I trust in my ability to make wise decisions that align with my highest good.

I release self-doubt and embrace self-confidence, knowing that I am capable of achieving greatness.

I am committed to my personal growth journey, investing in my well-being, and expanding my awareness.

I am grateful for every experience, as they have shaped me into the resilient and compassionate person I am today.

I am a source of inspiration and empowerment, lifting others up and encouraging them to embrace their own journey of healing and purpose.

Remember, affirmations are most effective when spoken with intention and belief. Repeat these affirmations daily, allowing them to permeate your consciousness and transform your mindset, helping you to release fear, heal from trauma, overcome pain, and step into a purposeful and fulfilling life.

# NO LONGER TRAPPED
## DEVOTIONS AND
## JOURNAL PROMPTS

Here are 7 daily devotions with corresponding scriptures from the Bible focused on healing, recovery, and God's grace, along with journal writing prompts for reflection:

# DAY 1:
# HEALING AND WHOLENESS

Scripture: "He heals the brokenhearted and binds up their wounds." - Psalm 147:3

### JOURNAL WRITING PROMPT:

Reflect on a past hurt or pain that still lingers within you. How can you surrender it to God and allow His healing to restore your heart? Write a prayer asking God to bring healing and wholeness to that area of your life.

_____

_____

_____

_____

_____

_____

_____

_____

_____

_____

## DAY 2:
## GOD'S COMFORT IN AFFLICTION

Scripture: "Blessed be the God and Father of our Lord Jesus Christ, the Father of mercies and God of all comfort, who comforts us in all our affliction, so that we may be able to comfort those who are in any affliction, with the comfort with which we ourselves are comforted by God." - 2 Corinthians 1:3-4

### JOURNAL WRITING PROMPT:

Think of a time when you experienced God's comforting presence in the midst of your affliction. How can you extend that same comfort to others who may be going through similar struggles? Write down practical ways you can offer comfort and support to someone in need.

_____

_____

_____

_____

_____

_____

_____

_____

# DAY 3:
# RENEWED STRENGTH

Scripture: "But those who hope in the LORD will renew their strength. They will soar on wings like eagles; they will run and not grow weary, they will walk and not be faint." - Isaiah 40:31

## JOURNAL WRITING PROMPT:

Consider an area in your life where you feel depleted or weary. How can you place your hope in the Lord and allow Him to renew your strength? Write about ways you can cultivate hope and find rejuvenation in God's presence.

_____

_____

_____

_____

_____

_____

_____

_____

_____

## DAY 4:
## GOD'S FAITHFULNESS IN RESTORATION

Scripture: "And after you have suffered a little while, the God of all grace, who has called you to his eternal glory in Christ, will himself restore, confirm, strengthen, and establish you." - 1 Peter 5:10

### JOURNAL WRITING PROMPT:

Reflect on a season of restoration or redemption in your life. How did God demonstrate His faithfulness during that time? Write a prayer of gratitude, thanking God for His restoring power and asking Him to continue strengthening and establishing you.

_____

_____

_____

_____

_____

_____

_____

_____

_____

## DAY 5:
## GOD'S PROMISES OF PEACE

Scripture: "Peace I leave with you; my peace I give you. I do not give to you as the world gives. Do not let your hearts be troubled and do not be afraid." - John 14:27

### JOURNAL WRITING PROMPT:

Consider an area in your life where you struggle to find peace. How can you lean on God's promise of peace and trust Him to calm your troubled heart? Write about steps you can take to cultivate a deeper sense of peace in that specific area.

_____

_____

_____

_____

_____

_____

_____

_____

_____

## DAY 6:
## GOD'S GRACE IN WEAKNESS

Scripture: "But he said to me, 'My grace is sufficient for you, for my power is made perfect in weakness.' Therefore, I will boast all the more gladly about my weaknesses, so that Christ's power may rest on me." - 2 Corinthians 12:9

### JOURNAL WRITING PROMPT:

Reflect on a personal weakness or inadequacy that often weighs you down. How can you embrace God's grace and allow His power to shine through your weakness? Write a prayer surrendering your weaknesses to God and inviting His strength to work in and through you.

_____

_____

_____

_____

_____

_____

_____

_____

_____

## DAY 7:
## GOD'S PLAN FOR RESTORATION

Scripture: "For I know the plans I have for you," declares the LORD, "plans to prosper you and not to harm you, plans to give you hope and a future " - Jeremiah 29:11

### JOURNAL WRITING PROMPT:

Consider an area of your life where you long for restoration and a fresh start. How can you trust God's plans and surrender your desires to His perfect timing? Write down your hopes and dreams, entrusting them to God's care and seeking His guidance for the future.

_____

_____

_____

_____

_____

_____

_____

_____

_____

_____

May these devotions and writing prompts encourage and inspire you as you seek healing, embrace recovery and experience the grace of God in your life.

# ABOUT THE AUTHOR

Dr. Shelita McGowan was born and raised in Kenner, Louisiana (outside of New Orleans). She graduated with a Bachelor of Science in Biology in 1998, as well as a Doctorate in Chiropractic in 2003. She is a practicing Chiropractor, wife, mom, sister, and friend to many. In addition to her career as a Chiropractor, Dr. Shelita has always had a passion for reading and writing for as long as she can remember. She also takes part in activities that help local area children.

Dr. Shelita not only demonstrates a passion for writing through her truth about experiencing and overcoming trauma, she is also committed to helping others overcome as well.

# About the Author

You can find out more about Dr. Shelita at www.mcgowansrc.com.

If you would like to connect with Dr. Shelita via social media, here are her contacts (she would love to hear from you!):

@Drshelita on Instagram

@Shelita Edwards-McGowan on Facebook

@ Shelita McGowan on LinkedIn

www.ingramcontent.com/pod-product-compliance
Lightning Source LLC
Chambersburg PA
CBHW041129110526
44592CB00020B/2743